BOYS

—

An Illustrated Field Guide

HEATHER ROSS

Abrams Image, New York

Editor: Tamar Brazis
Designer: Danielle Young
Production Manager: Denise LaCongo

Library of Congress Control Number: 2017930316

ISBN: 978-1-4197-2388-9

Printed and bound in the United States
10 9 8 7 6 5 4 3 2 1

Abrams Image books are available at special discounts
when purchased in quantity for premiums and promotions
as well as fundraising or educational use. Special editions can
also be created to specification. For details, contact
specialsales@abramsbooks.com or the address below.

ABRAMS The Art of Books

115 West 18th Street
New York, NY 10011
abramsbooks.com

For Bee and her cousins

There are lots of different types of boys.

CHAPTER 1

DANGEROUS BOYS

fig. 2

fig. 1

917
7558

fig. 3

Some boys are dangerous.

Dangerous Boys can be spotted easily,
because they want you to know
that they are Dangerous Boys.

Dangerous Boys make your heart beat fast.

Dangerous Boys are made of the same things as other kinds of boys, but also with scissors and matches and broken cups.

They can be identified by their Dangerous Boy hair
and Dangerous Boy clothes and Dangerous Boy vehicle.

Sometimes they will even have a Dangerous Boy pet.

fig. 4

fig. 5

fig. 6

fig. 7

fig. 8

fig. 9

Dangerous Boys will take you to exciting places and show you fearsome things.

You will feel afraid and brave and
strong when you are with them.

But always remember that a Dangerous Boy
will forget to keep you safe.

When you are with a Dangerous Boy,
you will need to be a Girl Who
Watches Out for Herself.

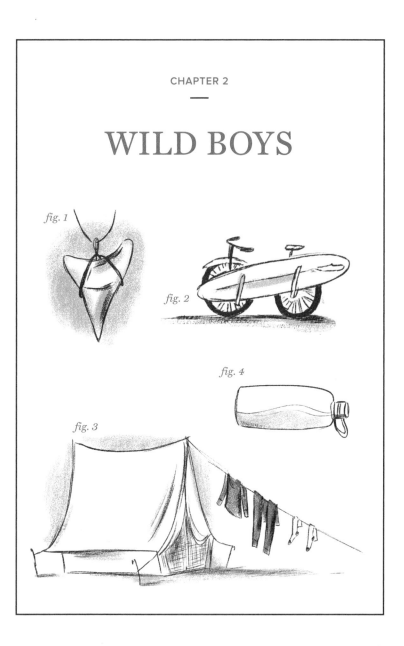

CHAPTER 2

WILD BOYS

fig. 1

fig. 2

fig. 4

fig. 3

Some boys are wild.

Wild Boys are made of sunrises and coyotes
and salt water.

They are often only seen in the early morning,
before they climb onto high wires or into the
green middle of a wave or another secret place
where time stops and everything else in
the everyday world disappears.

These are places that every girl should see,
and Wild Boys always know the way.

But Wild Boys will sometimes spend too much time in their secret places and forget that other things are important, too.

When you are with a Wild Boy, you will need to be
a Girl Who Can Find Her Own Way.

CHAPTER 3

SMART BOYS

fig. 1

fig. 2

1st
DEBATE

fig. 3

fig. 4

NIETZSCHE

Some boys are smart.

Smart Boys know a lot of things about a lot of things. This is because they are made with extra vitamin C and algebra.

They understand the very important things that
nobody can see, like atoms and radio waves . . .

. . . and the proper way to ice skate.

But when you are with a Smart Boy, it is important to be a Girl Who Questions Everything, including whether there is actually only one proper way to ice skate.

CHAPTER 4

BEAUTIFUL BOYS

fig. 1

fig. 2

SWOOOOP IT

fig. 3

KISS M

fig. 4

fig. 5

Some boys are beautiful.

Beautiful Boys are easy to spot, because they like to spend lots of time in places where girls like to be.

Beautiful Boys are made mostly of stars and chocolate and lightning.

Beautiful Boys have special magnets in their eyes that make you forget to breathe when they look at you. They make you believe they are looking for all of the most beautiful parts of you, the parts that nobody else can see.

But sometimes they are really just looking for their own reflections.

When you are with a Beautiful Boy, it is important to be a Girl Who Knows When to Close Her Eyes. You will let your *heart* see instead.

CHAPTER 5

—

QUIET BOYS

fig. 1

fig. 2

fig. 3

CONSTELLATIONS
AND
MYTHS

fig. 4

Some boys are quiet.

Quiet Boys can be the most difficult type of boy to notice, because they hide in the tall grass and moonlight and in the silent corners of lunchrooms and libraries.

They are made mostly of thoughts and deep water.
They don't talk very much, which makes them very
good at listening.

Quiet Boys are also good at knowing about other quiet things, like peace and falling stars and good books.

When you are with a Quiet Boy, it is important to be a Girl Who Knows How to Listen, because sometimes it takes a Quiet Boy a very long time to tell you his important things.

CHAPTER 6

BRAVE BOYS

fig. 1

LOCAL BOY SAVES CAT

fig. 2

SAVED THE

fig. 3

Brave Boys might be the best type of boy.

They are made of thick mud and shiny, round stones like the ones you find by the river.

Brave Boys are sometimes hard to find, because they look just like Regular Boys, until something scary happens.

Then there will be That Boy.
You will not see him coming.

But even if you had, it would not have mattered, because he will be made of sunlight and shivers and the air that you need to breathe.

It won't be on purpose, but he
might break your heart.

He will probably drop it accidentally, because he was not being careful enough or because he did not realize what he was holding or how fragile it was.

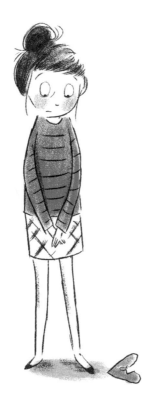

That will be awful.

That will be really, really, really awful.

It will feel like not having enough air to breathe.

It will feel like the sun has gone to the other side of the world.

It will feel like your hands and feet do not want to leave the ground.

You will not be able to imagine a time in the past or in the future when you will feel anything good at all.

But here's the thing about a heart.

It's made mostly of muscle, plus some extra strong rubber bands and other stretchy things. And tree forts and swing sets and butterflies and roller skates and rainstorms and waking up in the morning to see that it has snowed.

X-RAY

Free Kittens

SUPER BALL

And when it heals, which it will,
it will be stronger than before.

And bigger. And with more butterflies.

And you will have learned some new things, too.

You will have learned when to be quiet and when to be wild.

You will know the difference between acting dangerous and acting brave.

You will see what is truly beautiful.

You will be wise instead of just smart.

You will be a Girl Who Knows Herself.

And that will be the best love of all.